Easy Password [illegible]

Site	Username	Password

Easy Password Tracker

Site	Username	Password

Easy Password Tracker

Site	Username	Password

Easy Password Tracker

Site	Username	Password

Easy Password Tracker

Site	Username	Password

Easy Password Tracker

Site	Username	Password

Easy Password Tracker

Site	Username	Password

Easy Password Tracker

Site	Username	Password

Easy Password Tracker

Site	Username	Password

Easy Password Tracker

Site	Username	Password

Easy Password Tracker

Site	Username	Password

Easy Password Tracker

Site	Username	Password

Easy Password Tracker

Site	Username	Password

Easy Password Tracker

Site	Username	Password

Easy Password Tracker

Site	Username	Password

Easy Password Tracker

Site	Username	Password

Easy Password Tracker

Site	Username	Password

Easy Password Tracker

Site	Username	Password

Easy Password Tracker

Site	Username	Password

Easy Password Tracker

Site	Username	Password

Easy Password Tracker

Site	Username	Password

Easy Password Tracker

Site	Username	Password

Easy Password Tracker

Site	Username	Password

Easy Password Tracker

Site	Username	Password

Easy Password Tracker

Site	Username	Password

Easy Password Tracker

Site	Username	Password

Easy Password Tracker

Site	Username	Password

Easy Password Tracker

Site	Username	Password

Easy Password Tracker

Site	Username	Password

Easy Password Tracker

Site	Username	Password

Easy Password Tracker

Site	Username	Password

Easy Password Tracker

Site	Username	Password

Easy Password Tracker

Site	Username	Password

Easy Password Tracker

Site	Username	Password

Easy Password Tracker

Site	Username	Password

Easy Password Tracker

Site	Username	Password

Easy Password Tracker

Site	Username	Password

Easy Password Tracker

Site	Username	Password

Easy Password Tracker

Site	Username	Password

Easy Password Tracker

Site	Username	Password

Easy Password Tracker

Site	Username	Password

Easy Password Tracker

Site	Username	Password

Easy Password Tracker

Site	Username	Password

Easy Password Tracker

Site	Username	Password

Easy Password Tracker

Site	Username	Password

Easy Password Tracker

Site	Username	Password

Easy Password Tracker

Site	Username	Password

Easy Password Tracker

Site	Username	Password

Easy Password Tracker

Site	Username	Password

Easy Password Tracker

Site	Username	Password

www.ingramcontent.com/pod-product-compliance
Lightning Source LLC
Chambersburg PA
CBHW071553080326
40690CB00056B/1955
* 9 7 8 1 7 0 0 5 7 9 9 6 6 *